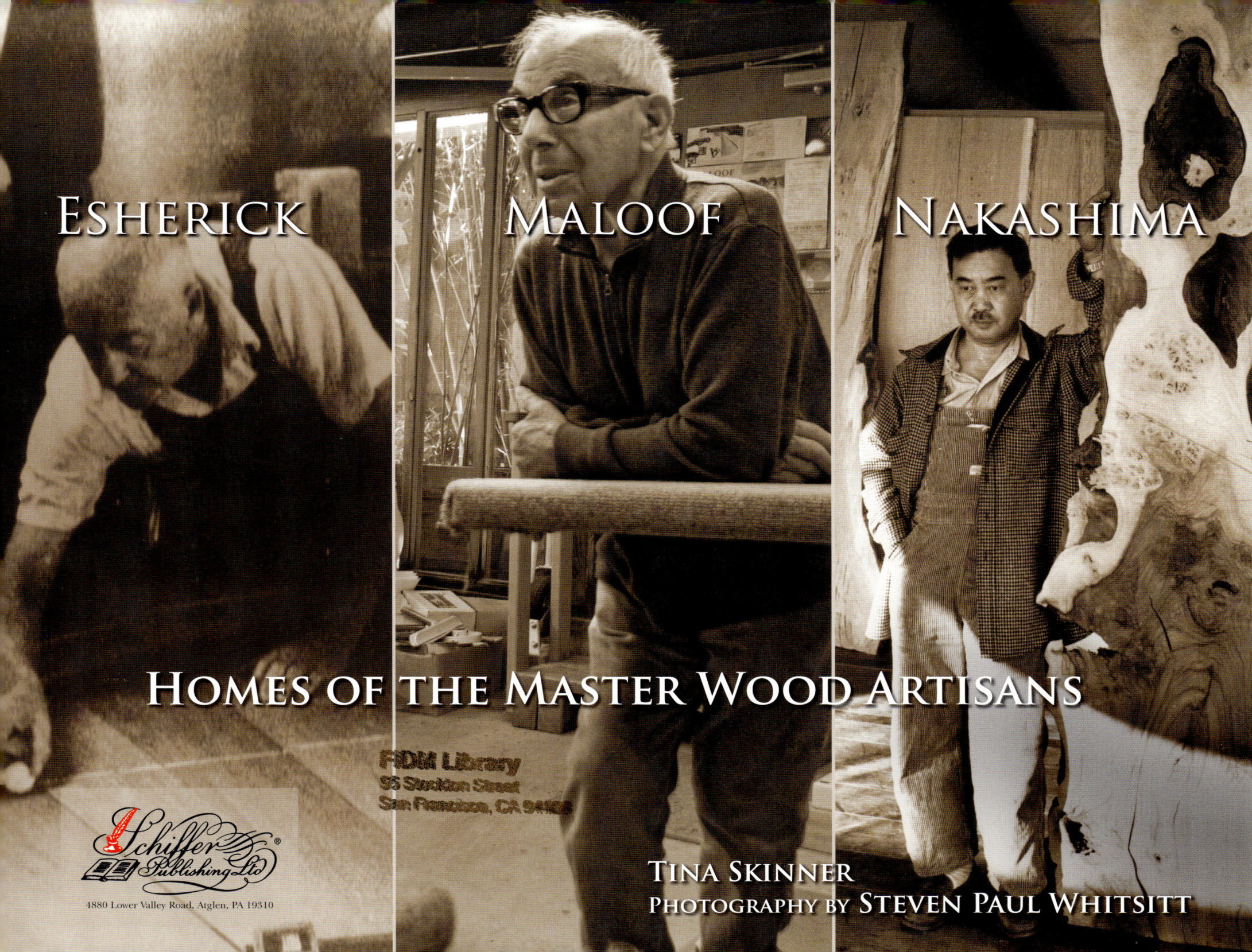

Esherick Maloof Nakashima

Homes of the Master Wood Artisans

Tina Skinner
Photography by Steven Paul Whitsitt

Schiffer Publishing Ltd
4880 Lower Valley Road, Atglen, PA 19310

Copyright © 2009 by Schiffer Publishing / Steven Paul Whitsitt
Library of Congress Control Number: 2008942474

All rights reserved. No part of this work may be reproduced or used in any form or by any means—graphic, electronic, or mechanical, including photocopying or information storage and retrieval systems—without written permission from the publisher.
The scanning, uploading and distribution of this book or any part thereof via the Internet or via any other means without the permission of the publisher is illegal and punishable by law. Please purchase only authorized editions and do not participate in or encourage the electronic piracy of copyrighted materials.
"Schiffer," "Schiffer Publishing Ltd. & Design," and the "Design of pen and ink well" are registered trademarks of Schiffer Publishing Ltd.

Designed by John P. Cheek
Cover design by Bruce Waters

Type set in TrajanPro/Adobe Jenson Pro/Humanist 521 Lt BT

ISBN: 978-0-7643-3202-9
Printed in China

Schiffer Books are available at special discounts for bulk purchases for sales promotions or premiums. Special editions, including personalized covers, corporate imprints, and excerpts can be created in large quantities for special needs. For more information contact the publisher:

Published by Schiffer Publishing Ltd.
4880 Lower Valley Road
Atglen, PA 19310
Phone: (610) 593-1777; Fax: (610) 593-2002
E-mail: Info@schifferbooks.com

For the largest selection of fine reference books on this and related subjects, please visit our web site at www.schifferbooks.com
We are always looking for people to write books on new and related subjects. If you have an idea for a book please contact us at the above address.

This book may be purchased from the publisher.
Include $5.00 for shipping.
Please try your bookstore first.
You may write for a free catalog.

In Europe, Schiffer books are distributed by
Bushwood Books
6 Marksbury Ave.
Kew Gardens
Surrey TW9 4JF England
Phone: 44 (0) 20 8392-8585; Fax: 44 (0) 20 8392-9876
E-mail: info@bushwoodbooks.co.uk
Website: www.bushwoodbooks.co.uk
Free postage in the U.K., Europe; air mail at cost.

TITLE PAGE IMAGES:
Left:
Wharton Esherick.
Courtesy of The Wharton Esherick Studio. Photograph by Robert Laurer, assistant director of the Museum of Contemporary Craft.

Center:
Sam Maloof.

Right:
George Nakashima.
Courtesy of George Nakashima Woodworker, S.A.

Contents

Acknowledgments _____ 4

Introduction _____ 5

Wharton Esherick (1887-1970) _____ 15

Sam Maloof (1916-) _____ 73

George Nakashima (1905-1990) _____ 115

Bibliography _____ 160

Acknowledgments

Three amazing institutions opened their doors, gave us complete access, plus smiles and warm welcomes to boot. We are awed by the graciousness, trust, and honor placed in us. Our most heartfelt gratitude to Robert Leonard, Paul Eisenhauer, Mansfield "Bob" Bascom, and Ruth Esherick Bascom at The Wharton Esherick Museum; to Roslyn Bock at the Sam and Alfreda Maloof Foundation for Arts and Crafts, and, of course, to Sam and Beverly Maloof; and to Mira Nakashima Yarnall, Kevin Nakashima, Jonathan Yarnall, and Soomi Amagasu at George Nakashima Woodworker, S.A.

Introduction

The mountaintop studio of Wharton Esherick.

This book offers an opportunity to enter homes created by three of the most important furniture craftsmen in modern American history. It's fascinating to see how the style of their homes reflects the thinking behind their furniture lines. Starting with the grandfather of the American Crafts Revival movement, Wharton Esherick, we enter a home where straight lines were avoided at all costs, and furniture took on creative, sculptural shapes hitherto not imagined. Esherick's mountaintop home and studio embodies his experimental nature and resourcefulness, as wood scraps became angled paneling and wending floorboards. Twigs and scraps became sculptural latches and locks. Now a museum, his work in mediums as broad as canvas and stone are on display within the framework of a wooden structure that empowers the imagination.

Sam Maloof, a hero among wood workers, built his success upon uncompromised commitment to the perfection of his furniture. His rambling complex of a home reflects his boundless energy, endless workdays, and constant desire to create. He has imbued every aspect of his

7,000-plus square feet of home with creativity, expressed in the furnishings, hinges, locks, and lovingly collected artworks. In his nineties, he's hard at work on another building now, and still refining his furniture designs.

In the home of George Nakashima, walls and windows connect inside and out, expressing his Japanese heritage and his admiration of nature. Likewise, the furniture he crafted is an expression of the wood he worked with, with much of the credit for the creation given to the tree. The book he wrote, *The Soul of a Tree*, is a meditation on the beauty and nature of the tree and a craftsman's role in helping the tree to express its joyful nature long after it has been cut down.

All three men embody a movement in woodworking that continues to influence today's fine craftsmen. At a moment in time when America and the industrial world were moving toward mass production, planned obsolescence, and escalating materialism, our three heroes intentionally set themselves apart, jealously guarding their independence and embracing their own economic uncertainty. All labored independently in pursuit of perfection, when they might have endeavored to patent designs and earn royalties from the manufacturing industry.

The postwar crafts movement or the American Crafts Revival movement of the 1960-70s differed from the Arts & Crafts movement of the 1920s and '30s. R. Craig Miller of the Metropolitan Museum of Art in New York wrote that the movement was not characterized

Wharton Esherick's library and bedroom.

Wharton Esherick's dining room.

by a defined style, but rather by a mindset. The artisans honored in exhibits and collections as part of this movement were noted for their dogged devotion to their style or medium, and their own expression.

The three men featured in this book inspired this new school of thought, featuring prominently in the exhibitions and mentoring a new generation of artisans. Each chose the medium of wood. Esherick, the eldest, expressed his wood artistry in furnishings and architecture as well as in abstract sculptures. Like him, Nakashima sought the unique potential among each piece of wood. Maloof, writing that he had no time to forge individual relationships with each piece of wood, labored intensively to refine and better his pieces, marrying comfort with design. All three forged their styles independently in creating practical, useful items that became part of the ongoing academic and aesthetic debate about the divide between art and craft.

In 1957, the first conference of American Craftsmen was held in Pacific Grove, California, attended by Maloof and Esherick. Maloof still recalls his meeting with Esherick and the empowerment it gave him. After a forum discussion in which Maloof heatedly asserted the necessity of a craftsman's skills to good design, and the value of a personal relationship with the customer for whom furniture was being designed, he was approached by Wharton Esherick, then seventy years old. "Young man," Esherick said, "stick to your convictions and don't stray from the way you work and believe. Remember what I've told you."

INTRODUCTION   7

All three of the artisans featured in this book lived their lives dedicated to their art and craft. Esherick was a renowned eccentric, isolated on a mountaintop near the Valley Forge battleground that earned its icy cold, rugged reputation during the American Revolution. His small home reflected his need to isolate himself and concentrate on his work, along with the meager finances of an artist who lives by inspiration, not commission.

Within miles, Nakashima led an artist's life that mirrored the perfection of every moment practiced by his Japanese ancestors, along with the reverence for the trees with which he worked. He created a complex of buildings where shoji screens blur the line between indoors and out, and frame nature as one of the primary adornments. His furnishings were a truly revolutionary style, in that the table and chairs he produced reserved the shape and celebrated the grain of the trees he worked with. Esherick and Nakashima met, though they never struck up a lasting friendship.

As in the earlier Arts & Crafts movement, the postwar crafts movement found a large audience in California, where craftsmen were recognized for providing the warmth of hands-on production for an upscale clientele. On the West Coast, Maloof managed to achieve a level of L.A. celebrity, and the complex of studio and living space he created in the shadow of the San Gabriel Mountains came to be celebrated nearly as much as his work. It was said that an average of 3,000 visitors toured his home annually before it was moved to make way for a freeway. Now

Left:
A 3" high music stand model by Wharton Esherick.

Right:
A music stand fashioned by Sam Maloof to accommodate a duet.

The original home of Sam Maloof grew organically, as he had money and time to create additions.

INTRODUCTION 9

relocated to a new complex, Maloof's home and workshop are museum exhibits with official hours for touring.

His home was "more like the idiosyncratic, highly personalized homes of fellow woodworkers Nakashima and Esherick, both of which Maloof had seen illustrated in magazines," wrote Jeremy Adamson in *The Furniture of Sam Maloof*. In the mid-1950s Maloof began to develop the "sculptural arms" that came to characterize his chairs. He sent images of some of these chairs to Wharton Esherick for review in 1958. Esherick, known as a wood sculptor, returned the images with a note: "I wish some of your things would have a little more sculptural quality." Maloof took the suggestion to heart.

A year later, en route to Lebanon, where he would design furniture for six months as part of a U.S. foreign assistance program, Maloof got an opportunity to view Esherick's work. On a stopover in Manhattan he visited the Museum of Contemporary Crafts where a ninety-piece retrospective of Esherick's work was on display. In his travel diary he wrote of Esherick's staircase, later crafting similar spirals for his homes.

Esherick, Maloof, and Nakashima were among the 267 artists represented in Objects: USA, a 1969 exhibition at the National Collection of Fine Arts that proved to be the museum's most popular exhibit. The exhibit went on a twenty-three-city tour, endeavoring to place American crafts on par with the fine arts. The three were also exhibited in the landmark 1971 exhibition *Woodenworks: Furniture Objects by Five Craftsmen* at the

A spice shelf fashioned by Sam Maloof.

A music stand by
George Nakashima

One of 14 buildings that blend into the nine-acre complex that Nakashima carefully cultivated within the natural environment of Eastern Pennsylvania

In creating his domestic environment, Nakashima bridged Eastern and Western cultures.

INTRODUCTION 13

Renwick Gallery of the Smithsonian, in company with Wendell Castle and Arthur Espenet Carpenter. Esherick passed away shortly before the exhibit.

Though their work had been exhibited side by side, Maloof and Nakashima didn't meet until the Californian dropped in at Nakashima's Pennsylvania studio in 1975. They became close friends with a deep respect for each other's work.

At this writing, Maloof is the last survivor of the three, still hard at work in his studio, attending parties, art-related functions, and receiving awards. All three men have left legacies in place that will survive generations. Esherick's studio is now a museum open for tours and changing lives one small group at a time. Nakashima's children, Mira and Kevin, continue his furniture making endeavors and open the showroom, finishing room, and studio for self-guided tours on Saturday afternoons. The George Nakashima House, Studio, and Workshop were listed on the U.S. National Register of Historic Places in August 2008. Previously, he created the non-profit Nakashima Foundation for Peace, www.nakashimafoundation.org.

The Sam and Alfreda Maloof Foundation for Arts and Crafts, a 501c3 non-profit organization, has been established to perpetuate excellence in craftsmanship, encourage artists, and make available to the public the treasure house the Maloofs lovingly created. Maloof's long-time assistants will carry on his work after he's gone since, at ninety-three years of age, he has nearly ten years of commissions before him.

Sliding doors and screens are carryovers from Nakashima's years of living in Japan.

Wharton Esherick
(1887-1970)

*Courtesy of The Wharton Esherick Studio.
Photograph by Connie Kanaga.*

This book presents the artisans in alphabetical order, and it is fortunate that Esherick falls first. He was born first, and many credit him with pioneering the creation of functional pieces that also find respect in art galleries and museums.

Esherick's own growth as an artist follows the unique forms of the early 20th century: Art Nouveau, Art Deco, Cubism, and finally finding his own unique style that put him at the forefront of a new craft revival movement that married fine art with function in the form of furnishings.

Esherick "is considered to be the most important furniture designer of the 20th century," writes the National Trust for Historic Preservation, the umbrella group that counts Esherick's studio among twenty model sites that preserve, document, and interpret Historic Artists' Homes and Studios.

Esherick is given a great deal of credit in art circles for the momentum and influence he provided for the studio furniture movement of the 1960s and '70s.

Esherick first attempted to find his medium in painting, studying drawing and printmaking first at the Philadelphia School of Industrial Art (now the University of the Arts) from 1907-1908 and then painting at the Pennsylvania Academy of the Fine Arts from 1909-10. He quit just six weeks before graduation, citing the need to develop his own style of painting over rote study of the masters.

Esherick found income creating posters for the Victor Talking Machine Company after he left college, but his service quickly became obsolete as technological advances allowed the use of photography. So, with his new bride, Letty Nofer, he moved to a farmhouse in Paoli and pursued painting full time. "She wanted to pursue an organic, rural life," relates Esherick's son-in-law, Mansfield "Bob" Bascom.

Esherick's first experiments in woodworking came in 1919 when he started to carve his frames to make his art more saleable. The frames flushed out his true calling, and before long he began to fashion woodcuts for magazine illustrations and nine books from 1921 through the mid-1930s. He began sculptural work in 1923. His first furniture came about in the mid-1920s as he sought to satisfy his own yearning for better furnishings in his own home. His early furniture was very much in the Arts and Crafts style popular at the time, with lots of carving and a heavy, medieval feel. "People who came to see his paintings wanted to buy his furniture," Bascom said. "So that's how he got into furniture making – expediency."

"Wharton's paintings received very little attention from galleries and museums," Bascom said. "When he got into sculpture, the people at the Whitney became interested. He realized that, if that was what got museums interested he'd better stick to the sculpture."

Esherick's isolated studio has contributed to his reputation as an isolated hermit. However, he was very involved in the arts scene, traveling to nearby Philadelphia and New York where he exhibited and cultivated a circle of arts and theater friends. His work was featured in many major exhibits during his lifetime, including shows at the Museum of Contemporary Craft in New York, the Museum of Modern Art in Philadelphia, the Tate Gallery in London, and the Art Institute of Chicago.

Having an isolated studio nurtured his prodigious productivity. He was fortunate to have several wealthy patrons who commissioned furnishings and even architectural elements like stairways and fireplaces that gave Esherick grand and celebrated spaces. Foremost among them was the home of Judge Curtis and Nellie Lee Bok of Gulph Mills, Pennsylvania, which was listed as one of the country's outstanding interiors by the *Brittannica Encyclopedia of American Art*.

Mostly, though, he scraped by. He worked primarily with woods close at hand, and had little contact with expensive, exotic materials. Moreover, much of his energy went into the creation of his own small but highly personal home.

Long after his death, Esherick continues to influence budding artists and craftsmen. Rob Leonard, Museum Executive Director, describes the effect that visiting the house has on those fortunate enough to make the trek to this Historic Landmark near Valley Forge. "I've seen people's lives changed," he writes. Formerly employed in "human services," he said that in the last nineteen years of working at the studio "I've done more human service here than ever before."

The collection at the studio: the home, the art, and the furniture on display, represents roughly twenty percent of his life's work. A tour of the home is an opportunity to see the varied interests and styles of a developing artist, and to marvel at the minute level of attention paid to every detail – from hand-carved coat pegs to cabinets and closets that light automatically when opened. Wharton's art encompassed every aspect of living – he fashioned plates, cutting boards, and other implements that adorned his kitchen. "Everything that you see was for sale," Bascom said. He'd have sold his bed – it would have given him the chance to make another bed!"

Esherick's wardrobe is still on display, neatly folded in drawers that smoothly glide about four feet back under his lofty, tree-top bed, where a self-fashioned reading lamp pulls into the perfect position to read propped up by pillows. Doors are perfectly balanced so that gentle pressure on one will make the other pop open. Every aspect of this petite house was crafted from a genius's eye for living, and a quest for craftsmanship.

All the energy that went into creating the home might not survive in a young man today, Leonard speculates. "They probably would have diagnosed him with (Attention Deficit Disorder). They would have 'fixed him' and he would have become a mundane businessman." Leonard relates how, to him, the life lesson Esherick left is "about following your heart."

Esherick's family was "gutsy and generous," he said, in creating The Warton Esherick Studio. Esherick's three children and many friends worked to create the museum. Esherick's daughter, Ruth Bascom, lives with her husband in the workshop Esherick built adjacent to the studio.

"Within two years of his death the doors were open. I'm still amazed," Rob Leonard said. The studio offers tours to small groups that must be booked by phone. "His son-in-law organized the tour program thirty years ago, and its still done the same way. All on a human scale," Leonard said. "Esherick set the tone and the family picked up on it. And the board of directors picked up on it too."

Wharton Esherick with assistant William McIntire working on the Dannenberg's table in 1958.

Courtesy of The Wharton Esherick Studio. Photograph by Robert Laurer, assistant director of the Museum of Contemporary Craft.

the life lesson Esherick left is "about following your heart."

Esherick was careful to avoid straight lines when he began work on his studio. He started with sturdy stone walls that flare at the base, like a tree growing out of the ground. He finished the main sandstone and oak section in 1926. A few years later he converted the lumber storage loft to a bedroom and moved in. In 1940 he added the tall wooden tower, which contains another bedroom and a dining area. A bathroom was added in 1947. The silo was built in 1966. He directed masons in the application of the colored concrete fresco, which mirrors the fall colors of the surrounding Pennsylvania countryside.

Esherick would frustrate the masons working on his studio by returning in the evening, after the workers had left, to scrape the mortar out from between the stones to create the more natural look he preferred.

A deck was one of the last additions to the home. Located off the dining room, it is a perfect example of Esherick's rejection of straight lines.

Built as a garage in 1928, the log structure was stained green and plum, using Wharton's favorite color combination. The garage is now home to a visitor's center where tours begin. The concrete building next door was created as a workshop in 1956, the design being a collaboration between Esherick and Louis I. Kahn. Wharton liked the way the concrete block created a dovetailed-like effect in the corners and insisted that they remain exposed.

A reception area in the main part of the home was where Wharton would receive guests and patrons. Oak beams salvaged from old barns create the great open space; the spiral pole is a piece of sculpture believed to have been inspired by Constantin Brancusi's *"Endless Column."* This room can take an hour on the tour, there is so much to see and absorb. Esherick's flowing sculptures are eye catchers. The couch is a telling example of Esherick's home planning – full drawers underline the seating area, making sure every inch of space is utilized. The bench next to it is a great example of the aesthetic Esherick gifted to subsequent craftsmen – the seat is formed by the wood itself, and there will never be another seat just like it. Esherick even crafted the lighting, shaping organic shades that focus the light beautifully.

A desk demonstrates the craftsman's great skill, each drawer a unique shape in the splayed pedestals. The shape was inspired by a sawhorse table Esherick witnessed at an artists' cooperative show in New York – where a craftsman played with a sawhorse table, putting the sawhorses upside down.

When Wharton delivered a commissioned dining table to a client, they found that the old sideboard looked out of place. They commissioned a new one from the artist, and sent him home with the old. Esherick painted it orange and black and made new handles for it. Atop it are, from the left: a model for a memorial competition, a model for a pipe holder, "Flame," a model for a sculpture tree on a stair landing, a model for a gravemarker for Sherwood Anderson, and "Centaur," a part from a bookstore sign.

A wood carving by Esherick looks as though it was acquired in Southeast Asia. Esherick's work and scope is always surprising. Called My Zhar Ptitsa, it first served as a grille between the studio and workshop in the farmhouse down the hill.

An early cabinet by Esherick was inspired by his rustic surroundings. The trees outside his studio were said to inspire the relief carvings on the face of this desk, while the top lines are abstract representations of turkey buzzards soaring above.

A small cabinet of curly oak appears artful, almost modest in a corner of the gallery room. Opened, however, it testifies to the great genius of Esherick. Flat workspaces draw out, with paperwork stored flat and easy to find on the many work surfaces. Above, two box lights pull out, turning on automatically when drawn upon. The stool is one of Esherick's trademark pieces. He created hundreds of these pieces, often crafting them from scraps found in the neighboring woods. No two are alike.

Next to the ingenious work center, a collection of furniture showcases trademark Esherick design. The semi-circular seat was his "club bench, allowing several people to warm their backs at the fire." His self-portrait hangs beside them, a memento of his first pursuit as a painter. Black and white photographs record his work, including his own famous stair on the left.

30   WHARTON ESHERICK

A music stand. Like most of Esherick's work, the observer is challenged to find a straight line or a 90-degree angle.

Double doors allowed Esherick to move large pieces in and out of the studio. However, they are testaments to his art. The latch, fashioned from ebony, is typical of his innovation. The eagle above was salvaged during a restoration project at the Academy of Music.

Wharton's hand is evident where his hands went — on the bolts and latches of his doors.

Esherick's famous stair was actually dismantled and taken to the World's Fair in New York in 1940 and again to New York City for an exhibit at the Museum of Contemporary Craft in 1958. Fashioned from heavy slabs of red oak, the steps were tenoned into the sculpted center post and bolted in. When climbing the spiral, which ascends almost ten feet, you have a choice of branching off on a separate set of steps that leads to the silo and the kitchen and dining areas. A mastodon tusk forms one handrail. "the handles on the stairs are exactly where you need them, and they fit the hand perfectly," marvels Bascom.

WHARTON ESHERICK 37

Details from the stair.

Esherick carved a number of abstract horses, like this one stained purple. One of his paintings of Mary, age eight, overlooks the landing over a short flight of massive timber stairs.

Carved light switches.

A fanning of floorboards adds poetry to a passageway under the stairs.

42 WHARTON ESHERICK

On the wall a row of coat pegs characterizes the workmen who helped Esherick build the tower addition on his home.

A small business center is tucked under the stairs, with a self-fashioned paper dispenser for messages, and a tuck-away drawer designed for the phone book. This was before the time of phone extensions, so the phone was located at the center of the house, an equal run from all directions.

The kitchen is curved like the silo it occupies. Esherick's hand-carved cutting boards and bowls are on display, as is his collection of Mexican glassware. The cabinets open with finger pulls because Esherick hated the way knobs predominated on furniture designs. Many of them light automatically when opened.

Esherick's hand is on every inch of his kitchen, from the utensils to the special features like a hand-fashioned shelf or windowsill.

48 WHARTON ESHERICK

The mosaic floorboard in the dining area was crafted from cherry, harvested from branches on an old tree that died on the property. The wall paneling and ceiling were set at angles, and overlapped, so that every viewpoint is fascinating, including Esherick's window, which looks out over the woods that nurtured his creative spirit.

The dining table seated four or five. Note the lighting that he crafted. A beautiful wood shade is suspended from a swinging arm over the table. A recycled copper pot lid shields a bare bulb over the back door to the right. This image is a good opportunity to observe the varied lines in the paneling, and the overlap of the rough-sawn ceiling planks.

A forked branch was lovingly sculpted to support a shelf in Esherick's home. Above, a cast sculpture, called "*Her*," gazes out the window. The original figure, made of wood, is in the bedroom. The "No" figure, cast in brass, was made for the Hedgerow Theater.

An angled mirror reflects Esherick's sense of humor, while adding light and space to the narrow dining area. The framed piece on the wall reflects Esherick's humor as well. When a customer returned with a wastebasket, claiming it was too tall, Esherick cut off the top and used the leftover piece as a wall hanging. A frying pan handle adorns the fanciful frame.

Esherick's lofty bedroom is a testament to his practicality, with bare stonewalls and an inexpensive, Celotex® siding used in the walls and ceiling. Rag rugs provide scant comfort. Bookshelves predominate, and a great, tapered, curved shelf in the far corner attests to the owner's subtle artistry.

A high bed is where Esherick fed his voracious appetite for books. Florescent lights swing out on a hinged arm, and tuck away when not in use. The bed is at window height with a southern view.

Storage under the bed is enviable. Perfectly balanced drawers run the full width of the bed, and pull all the way out for easy visual access to the contents. Esherick's wardrobe still rests neatly folded within.

A dresser was a commission piece. He thought flat drawers would make finding clothing easier. It was rejected by the client, who couldn't afford it.

The trap door lowers easily, using a carved wooden figure of his daughter, Mary, as a counterweight.

A trap door could be lowered and raised to seal off the loft from the sometimes-dusty work area below. Esherick converted this area to a bedroom and moved in after he and his wife separated.

Another view of the loft bedroom looks out through the north light dormer windows that face the entrance.

This library ladder is a much-celebrated Esherick piece. The steps climb a naturally spiraling post that turns back at the top, fitting the hand just right.

Stone ledges in the sculpture well were created in 1959, when Esherick discovered termites under his floor and concluded that digging out the lower level was the best way to ensure that they were eradicated. Today the well it is a wonderful gallery for works by Esherick.
(continued on following 3 pages)

64 WHARTON ESHERICK

Examples of his woodcuts are also on display along with a printing press he used.

A replica of Esherick's outhouse was recently reconstructed for the studio and is housed in his old woodshed.

Esherick's daughter and her husband, Mansfield "Bob" Bascom, are devoting their retirement years to the preservation of Esherick's work and artistic legacy. They refurbished and moved into his workshop area, an inspiring space designed by Esherick with architect Louis I. Kahn.

The Bascom's home is furnished primarily with pieces by Esherick. In 1980 they received a call from the executive director of the Cornell Museum. Esherick patron Dr. Harold More had left his collection of Esherick furniture to the museum, but it wasn't considered old enough to qualify for their collection. The Bascom's quickly brought it home for the collection they tend. The sculpture behind the couch is "Adolescence," a nude girl caught unawares. Her lower half is reflected in the Esherick's dining room floorboards.

The work area that used to house Esherick's joiner and planer is now a small conservatory in the Bascom home. Esherick's sculpture, *Reverence*, previously exhibited in both the Philadelphia Museum of Art and the New York Museum of Art, overlooks the lush space.

The shop is composed of three hexagons. Each hexagon has diamond-shaped roof planes, with beams that go in different directions in each plane. Wharton added curves to the walls as the structure was being built, though he had to keep the southern walls with windows straight.

Sam MALOOF
(1916-)

Sam Maloof is America's most renowned contemporary furniture craftsman. "No other twentieth-century woodworker has received such attention in the media, nor garnered as many awards," wrote Jeremy Adamson in *The Furniture of Sam Maloof*. He has rubbed elbows with move stars and presidents (both in the case of Ronald Reagan) and counts Jimmy Carter, a fellow woodworker, among his dear friends. Awards and certificates are stacked up on the floor in his home for want of wall space, including an Honorary doctor of the arts from Rhode Island School of Design, and awards from the American Institute of Architects, the American Craft Council, California Historical Society, and the John D. And Catherine T. MacArthur Foundation In the collections of the Carter Presidential Library and the White House.

Carter wrote a letter to him on November 15, 2001, congratulating Maloof on his Smithsonian exhibit: "Now even more of the world will have the chance to delight in your unparalleled talent as America's most celebrated furniture craftsman… Your passion for life, and for your craft, is obvious in every piece of your exquisite furniture."

Despite waxing and waning popularity among designers, curators, celebrities, and wood workers, Sam Maloof has steadily kept at what he loves – carefully crafting furniture by hand, every piece designed and supervised by himself and assisted by only a miniscule staff. And though he has willingly traveled to teach and to promote, he has cultivated a happy cocoon in the countryside, surrounded by family in an environment he conceived, built, and cultivated in his own fashion. "I do fantasize about building a small, perfect house where all the woodwork is beautifully shaped," Maloof wrote, but admitted that he hasn't had time to build his home the way he builds his furniture.

In his autobiography, *Sam Maloof: Woodworker*, he recalls that from childhood he was always creating things. He experimented with woodcarving as a young man, and took a strong interest in the arts. He pursued jobs working for an architect and an industrial designer before being drafted into the Army. Even there, he found a niche for himself drawing the company mascot and sketching out gun placements for his colonel.

After his stint in the Army, Maloof went to work as a graphic artist at a decal company that had reproduced some of his wartime drawings. Perhaps he can blame the poor pay of an entry-level artist for his future success.

"While I worked there I lived in a little furnished apartment. The furniture was awful. I enrolled in night school to use the machinery to make furniture so that I could stand living in the place," he wrote. A friend admired his furniture, and told him people would probably buy it.

The seed was planted, but Maloof went on to more jobs. He next worked for Millard Sheets, who headed the art departments at both Scripps and Claremont Colleges.

While working for Sheets he met his wife, Alfreda Ward, in 1947. She was studying for her masters of fine arts degree at Claremont Graduate School. "We were married immediately, just like that," Maloof wrote. The story of Sam Maloof would be incomplete without Freda, a woman he describes as "a true partner" and "very close."

Alfreda had been director of arts and crafts at the Santa Fe Indian School. When her father died she returned home to California and bought a small home for her mother and herself. She was accepted for admission to the Claremont Graduate School, where Sam met her.

The newlyweds moved into a small GI Loan house, and had very little furniture. Freda fixed up some lemon crates to look quite nice, Maloof says, and he began woodworking in their single-car garage.

A friend gave him some plywood that had been used to form concrete. He had them sandblasted, which created a beautiful etched grain look, and created a dining room and living room furniture that turned out so well it was photographed for *Better Homes and Gardens*. The magazine also commissioned drawings of the furniture so that they could sell the patterns. The $150 payment "seemed like $150,000" at that time, Maloof wrote. Encouraged by that money, and the interest generated by the article, he left his job to make furniture full time. In ensuing years the two lived on little as he grew the business, and Freda, ever supportive, meticulously recorded every piece that Maloof made.

The leap from the tiny suburban L.A. tract house photographed for the national magazine to a lemon grove further out into the rural San Gabriel Mountain region was a huge commitment on the part of the struggling family. "I kept talking about moving out to the country," Maloof relates, telling how Freda finally told him, in 1951, "Why don't we do it? I'm tired of hearing you talk about it."

That evening he looked through the paper and found a two-acre property in the foothills of Mt. Baldy. The property had a farmer's shack and a chicken coop, redeemed by the ancient avocado tree on site. It took three months to work out a deal Maloof could afford, when the owner accepted the $3,000 in equity the couple had in their current house as a down payment on the $9,500 property. Later they acquired another three acres next door.

They lived in the shack, and Maloof worked out of the chicken coop, which was so low that he could not stand up straight inside. Soon he poured a concrete slab for a new shop, but for a while he worked outside on the slab, moving his tools back into the chicken coop at night.

He broke ground for a new house in 1954, adding rooms to the house that grew, and grew.

"My environment is a wonderful one, but again, it is something that was created by hand. The making of it is even more satisfying than sitting back and enjoying the finished product," Maloof wrote in his book. "The whole thing – the house, the grounds, the workshop – is to me a reflection of how Freda and I feel about life and living. I hope it spells out joy to others."

Throughout his career, Maloof has found his audience shifting. He got his first commissions from designers and architects and then, increasingly, art collectors. "In the 1980s, as crafts became increasingly 'artified' and the market for unique forms boomed, Maloof's practical designs and traditional techniques found a more appreciative audience among amateur cabinetmakers… To the legions of cabinetmakers active in basement workshops across North America, he was a woodworking hero," wrote Adamson. "His autobiography, *Sam Maloof: Woodworker* (1983), proved an inspirational best-seller, as did the instructional, hour-long videotape, *Sam Maloof: Woodworking Profile* (1989).

In the latter years of his life, Maloof's work is sought by collectors willing to wait up to ten years for their commissions to be fulfilled. Maloof still designs every piece, and takes a hand in the entire process of production. "If we do 40 pieces a year we feel we've done really well," he said.

"Sam Maloof is one of only a handful of furniture designer-craftsmen active after 1945 to make his livelihood through working full time with his hands," wrote Jeremy Adamson in *The Furniture of Sam Maloof*

"My home, my shop, and my family are very important to me, both on a personal level and as an environment for work. I have often wondered what I would do if I had to drive to work in an industrial area…When I drive into Los Angeles, I am completely exhausted by the time I return home, but I can work in my shop until midnight and it does not bother me a bit," Maloof wrote.

The threat of a coming freeway loomed over the Maloof family for many years before it actually happened. Before the final word, Maloof wrote that "Consequently I have changed some of my plans because I figured, if the freeway should go through, why spend so much time and money on the house. About three additions back, I decided not to build a big 35 x 18 foot room and instead built a smaller room."

While the reality of the coming freeway was bearing down on them, Freda and Sam were active in traveling, receiving accolades around the country, and hordes of curious visitors at home. In the 1990s, more than 3,000 visitors a year would drop in, invariably receiving a warm reception and leaving in awe of the magic the Maloofs created.

Freda did not live to see the new house and studio completed in 2000. Her health was fragile, and she passed away in 1998 after suffering a massive heart attack in her sleep. She was eighty-six years old, and had been married to Maloof for fifty years.

She was, however, instrumental in planning the Maloof Foundation, a non-profit that promotes excellence in craftsmanship, encourages artists, and makes their home and art collection available to the public. More information is available online at www.malooffoundation.org.

Maloof has started his new life in the new house. "I like the other house an awful lot," Maloof says, noting that he and his new wife, Beverly, "go up there once in a while to sleep."

Besides constant vigilance over two large homes, Maloof is still busy overseeing the production of commissioned furniture from his workshop. He has several assistants who have been with him many years and who are expected to carry on after he passes. He also greets tour groups as affably as he has throughout his life. Maloof is someone who is an instant friend, ready to teach and share with anyone who's interested.

"People want furniture that they can sit on that is comfortable. They can also be well designed. I do care about how they look, very much so, or I wouldn't take all the time I do."

"*My environment is a wonderful one, but again, it is something that was created by hand. The making of it is even more satisfying than sitting back and enjoying the finished product.*"

Bob Stocksdale gave an electric wood-burning pen to Maloof in the early 1970s. Previously he had used a brand on his pieces, but he switched to the pen for a special exhibit at the Renwick Gallery in 1971, inscribing each of eight pieces he designed for the show with his name, the year, the Renwick Gallery. He has employed the pen for the rest of his career, numbering pieces sequentially each year and employing the calligraphic skills he developed in high school.

Maloof with Larry White, his first employee.

"Sometimes we have people walking around trying to find the front door," Maloof wrote of the house that grew on his little country property. "It does not have a front, back, or sides because I have always felt a house should be a monolith: it should look handsome regardless of the angle from which you approach it… I do not use drawings when I am adding on to the house. I just hold up a two-by-four and think, 'That looks pretty good,' and then nail it up. I do it all by eye." His executive assistant, Roslyn Bock, describes it a little differently: "It grew like popcorn," she said.

Visitors arriving at the Maloof Foundation enter a courtyard from the parking lot. A bell tower and a decorative redwood gate create architectural awe. The garden surroundings reflect the garden atmosphere that has long been credited with inspiring and nurturing Maloof's creativity and work ethic.

A wood storage shed is one of the facades that cradle the courtyard area. It seems right at home in its California setting. It is adorned with the fronts of old fruit crates. Maloof helped pay for his original rural property with the proceeds from the lemon trees that grew there.

Original rooms in the home reflect both the couple's early financial struggles, as well as the lower profile and smaller scale that was part of mid-century design. The couple's first floors were un-mortared brick that would shift slightly when walked on. Maloof called them "singing floors." Here the original floor underlies the core area of the home – open spaces connecting kitchen, dining, and living areas of the home. The couple's love of the Southwest is reflected in the color scheme, along with the extensive collection of Pre-Columbian pottery and North American Indian textiles and pottery, along with the eclectic accumulation of artwork from friends and associates throughout the years.

Woodworking skills are on display in this kitchen, as well as a straightforward practicality.

An informal dining area in the kitchen is, like the rest of the home, crowded with loved art.

On the other side of the kitchen counter, an expanded dining area was used for entertaining.

The bronzed hands of Sam on the dining table were presented by the faculty and students of Palomar College.

SAM MALOOF

A passageway beyond the dining room was bumped up to tower proportions. It adds to the profile of the house from outside, and creates a wonderful place to showcase unpainted carousel horses below.

"I got carried away designing our bedroom," Maloof wrote, noting that the room measures 20 x 36 feet. Even when Sam and Freda shared this room, it was filled with collected treasure. Now a glass display case, and even the bed, house and exhibit their collected artworks.

SAM MALOOF   89

Built as a two-story office and studio for Freda in 1975-1976, this space had become a showroom/gallery by 1990 by the time the freeway project was approved. The laminated, carved spiral staircase, added in 1997, was fashioned from packing case wood used to transport sport boats from Taiwan. The stained glass above the door spells "Alfreda."

Because it functions as a museum, adjustments have been made, like the addition of exit signs, alarms, and fire and evacuation signs. Still, it's an incredible opportunity to observe the work of a master craftsman, to actually work his latches and move through environments that he created.

Found logs provide support beams in a guest room, lightly finished to preserve the story of their creation. Few significant southern California artists lack representation in the extensive collection of art Sam Maloof has collected through the years.

Matching doors reveal the care of a meticulous wood craftsman.

A music room features one of many music stands designed and built by Sam Maloof, as well as an assortment of his comfortable furnishings.

Music stands are found throughout the home.

96 SAM MALOOF

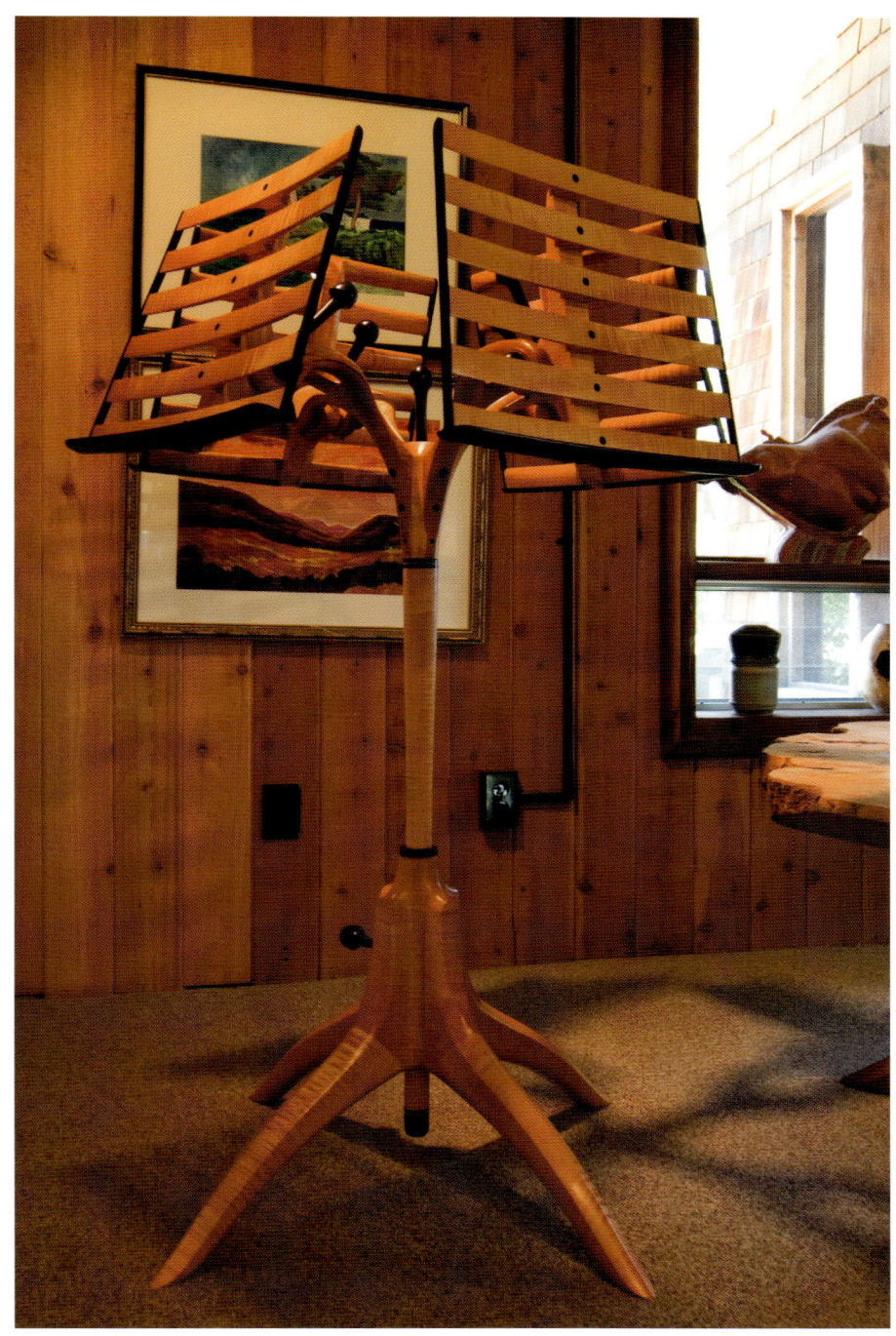

Two convenient shelves double as wall art.

98 SAM MALOOF

This is California – doors open directly to the semi-arid outdoors, without concern for screens to keep out mosquitoes, or huge overhangs to protect exposed wood from precipitation. Maloof exercised his creativity in creating novel doors throughout his home.

Stained glass is framed in fine woodwork on French doors that opened to the former gallery. Hinges and the latch are wonderful examples of one-of-a-kind craftsmanship.

100   SAM MALOOF

SAM MALOOF 101

102　sam MALOOF

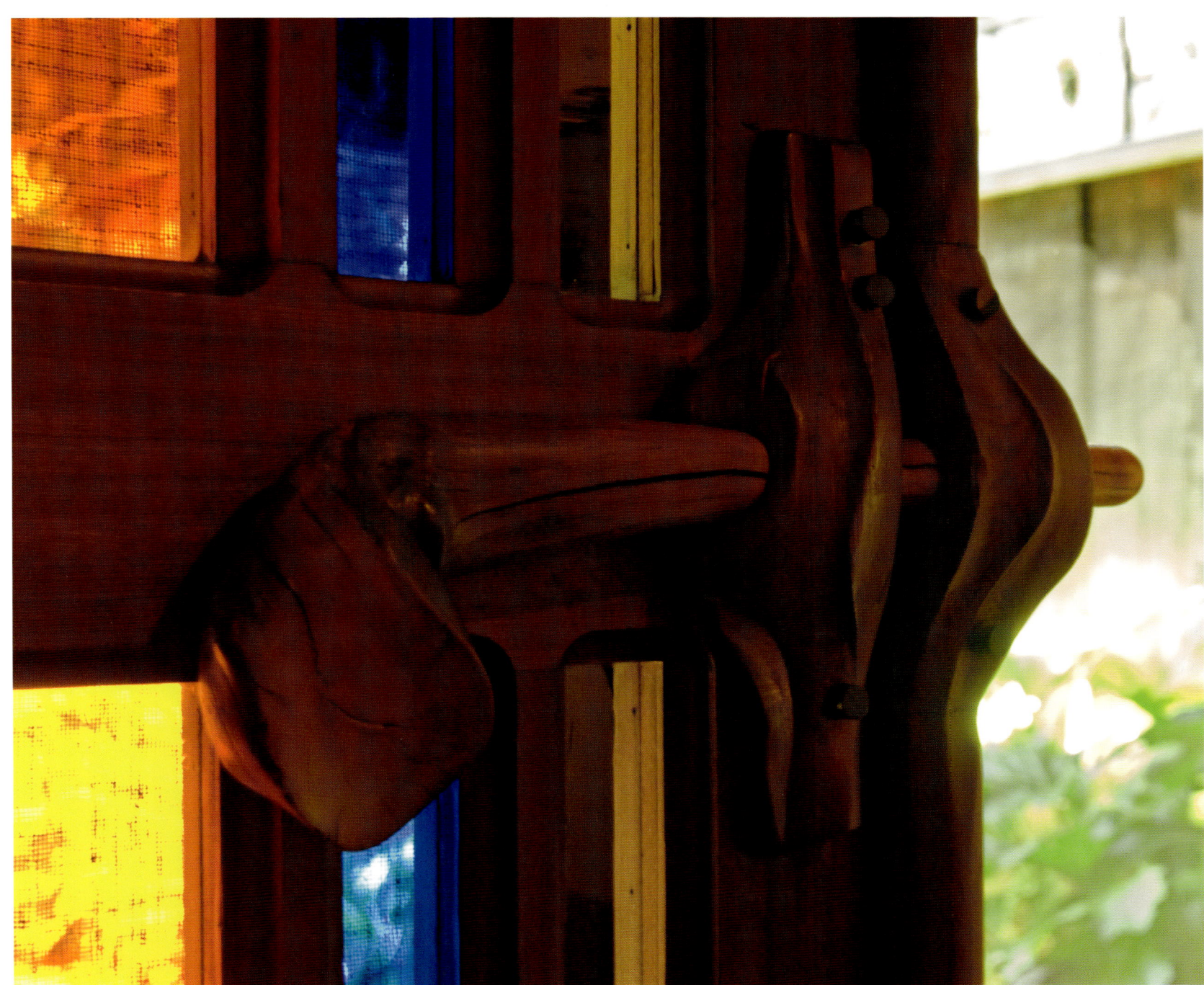

Like his mentor Wharton Esherick, Maloof allowed a found piece of wood to become art in its own right, following its natural form when creating a latch.

Examples of crafted hinges and latches that adorn doors in the original Maloof house. "Making latches is a great deal of fun for me," Maloof wrote. "Each door in our home has a different kind." (continued on following 3 pages)

SAM MALOOF 107

A wall hook.

108 SAM MALOOF

The tree top room was added in the mid-1980s. The roof beam is non-structural, but is a wonderful memento of a eucalyptus tree branch that fell while the room was being built.

SAM MALOOF 109

The original home continues in its endless transformation. The wallboards shown are not yet installed. Maloof rushes over before we take this picture and straightens them a bit, explaining that he is at work creating this wall. The blue door at the right opens to a large room that is being used for storage, and Maloof is planning its restoration.

Maloof crafted the spiral staircase in the new home that is the centerpiece of the central living area.

THE NEW HOUSE

His new home is as open to visitors as the old one just up the hill. Maloof happily invites visitors in, but apologizes as they cross the threshold that he doesn't really like it. He didn't build it himself. He has plans to change it, to make kitchen cabinets himself. Nonetheless, the home is still of his design. He did drawings for the architects who hammered out the details, and even had his assistant, Larry White, create a scale model to make sure the frame and structure were much as he wanted.

The master bedroom in the new house is a wonderful exhibition of Maloof's casework, he is best known for his chairs. Maloof's collecting continues unabated. The Foundation hosts art and craft shows, and Beverly is forever searching for space to house Sam's new art acquisitions.
(continued on following 3 pages)

George Nakashima
(1905-1990)

*Courtesy of The George Nakashima Archives.
Photograph by Osamu Murai.*

In the world of fine woodworking, George Nakashima spearheaded a movement in which the natural form of wood dictates the form of furnishings. His house and the other buildings he built near New Hope, Pennsylvania, marry the aesthetic of Japanese design and the nature of a three-acre oasis in Pennsylvania. His property embodies his desire to lead a life close to nature.

Nakashima's life reads like a great saga, with a soul-searching quest, true love, and the discovery of true purpose. Fortunately he has recorded his story in *The Soul of a Tree*, a must-read to truly know him, his sincerity, and earnestness.

In writing about his youthful adventures in the forests and mountains of the Pacific Northwest it is hard to imagine how he ever tore himself from the wilderness. Born to Japanese immigrants, he worked on the railroad and in salmon canneries to pay for his education. He worked summers, and studied architecture at the University of Washington. He is quite humble in glazing over a college career that took him to the Massachusetts Institute of Technology for postgraduate studies, along with a stint at the Fountainebleau in Paris to study architecture in 1928.

Then he began a seven-year "vagabondage" around the world. He spent the first year of the journey in Paris, then a hub of creative energy. Then he went to Japan for five years, where he visited family and eventually went to work in the Tokyo architectural offices of Antonin Raymond, an American who had come to Japan to work with Frank Lloyd Wright in the early 1920s and then stayed on. When the call went out for an architect to go to Pondicherry, India, to design and construct the main building of the Sri Aurobindo Ashram, Nakashima volunteered, literally. He refused salary and lived for two years as a devotee while building the ashram. This is where he fashioned his first pieces of furniture.

Japan and China were at war when Nakashima left India. During his six-month stay in Japan, he met Marion, they were married in Los Angeles, and she followed him back to Seattle in 1941. Touring the West Coast, Nakashima was uninspired by contemporary architecture and what he considered shoddy workmanship. He decided he would pursue woodworking, and began to make furniture and teach woodworking in Seattle. The pursuit was put on hold, however, when he was put in an internment camp following the attack on Pearl Harbor. In the Idaho camp, Nakashima worked with Gentaro Hikogawa, a Japanese-trained carpenter, designing and crafting pieces from scraps of wood and bitterbrush found in the nearby desert. When the rules for internment relaxed, Nakashima found a sponsor in Antonin Raymond, who owned a farm in Pennsylvania. He was released to go work on the farm, though after a year he concluded that this was not the work for him, that he was not compatible with chickens. He struck out on his own, staying in the New Hope area north of Philadelphia.

At first he rented a house and began to design and make furniture. Soon a landowner offered him three acres in barter for work, a "great act of generosity," Nakashima writes. In the beginning they actually lived in a tent. "Like the farmer who first builds his barn, we built our workshop first," he said. "At no time did we have more than fifty dollars in cash, but by scrounging materials, gathering stones off the property, digging foundation by hand, and working evenings and weekends, I was able to build a rough structure," he writes. That structure and the three acres surrounding it has grown and transformed with prosperity and need. "As our affairs improved, we added buildings when needed," Nakashima wrote. "To satisfy my original interest in architecture, I have designed and built six roofs of different warped forms on our property: three hyperbolic paraboloids, and three conoidal forms of different materials and shapes."

"My father was always, at heart, an architect," wrote Mira in *Nature, Form, and Spirit*. "As the business prospered it afforded him the financial capability to consider building again. 1954 marked the beginning of a flurry of building. 1956-67 were the most inspired and prolific and innovative years in my father's life."

There are fifteen buildings on the property, all built by George Nakashima, except the wood storage building. The showroom was built in 1954; the chair department in 1956; the finishing room in 1956. The Conoid Studio was started in 1957, finished in 1960.

"It has been nice to go it alone, to forge a life in the wilderness, to fight against commercialism and bigness," Nakashima said. "We have managed to bypass the whole money system, having never had a mortgage and practically nothing in the way of loans, perhaps like the early English Quakers who built so splendidly on this land."

George Nakashima at work in the Conoid Studio. *Courtesy of George Nakashima Woodworker, S.A.*

George and Marion Nakashima in their home.
Courtesy of George Nakashima Woodworker, S.A.

"Like the farmer who first builds his barn, we built our workshop first."

Daughter Mira in the family home, 1950.
Courtesy of George Nakashima Woodworker, S.A.

Jonathan Yarnall, George Nakashima's son-in-law, said that when Japanese people come to the complex, they comment that, "this is what it was like in Old Japan. There's not much of that left." Nakashima's aesthetic marries architecture to the environment.

Nakashima finished the Conoid Studio in 1960. The roof was poured with 2-1/2 inch thick reinforced concrete. "I remember when he was knocking the support out," Mira recalls. "He would do it himself. He would knock off a support and run around and make sure it was still standing. He was exalted, I'm sure." The southern facade is sited for maximum passive solar gain in the winter, its facade of glass and shoji doors providing visual variation. "Building the Conoid Studio was a true adventure," Nakashima wrote. "The arching roof—a double reverse conoid – was a complete experiment. It took ten yards of concrete (each yard weighing about three tons to pour the roof, which is only a thin shell two-and-a-half inches thick. The engineering was done by Mario Salvadori. The span is forty by forty feet, but no beams or poles support the roof. The entire weight rests on the concrete arch on the south side of the building and the back wall."

Furnishings and prized wood slabs are on display for visitors who attend open houses at the Nakashima studio.

A reception area inside the Conoid studio is warmed by a bank of southern facing windows.

A display of unusual knots and burls, which Nakashima often used to create his lamp bases, door pulls and handles.

Customers wishing to commission furniture visit the design offices in the Conoid Studio, where furniture samples, as well as wood samples, are on display.

The Conoid studio looks out over the woods Nakashima loved so much. The back has a scalloped roofline.

GEORGE NAKASHIMA

A reception area and offices sit centrally within the compound. Inside, a seating area hosts guests who come for appointments to design their custom-made furniture.

The Minguren Museum was an ambitious experiment by Nakashima in building a hyperbolic paraboloid shell roof – meaning that curves run in two directions across the roof. As Jonathan Yarnall explains it, "the tension of the curve controls the roof. There's very little support of the peak. There's stone and tar on top of three layers of plywood – quite a bit of weight unsupported.

Nakashima dug a number of holes in the ground to act as ponds. They filled naturally with water and have become home to frogs and plant life. They occasionally require some refilling, says Jonathan Yarnall, but are mostly self-sustaining.

Artist Ben Shahn observed the flat wall at the base of the Minguren Museum and told his friend that a mural was needed. Shahn provided a drawing. After the artist died, Nakashima and his son Kevin took the drawing to the Gabriel Loire Atelier in Chartres, France, where it was interpreted into a mosaic on eight large panels and then shipped over. "Ben Shahn was my father's best friend and favorite artist," said Kevin. "He was my adopted grandfather at one point. They used to exchange furniture for paintings." Ben Shahn has been the subject of a PBS documentary and at least seven books have been written about him and his work.

A homey seating area in the Minguren Museum opens directly to the outdoors via shoji screens.

GEORGE NAKASHIMA

There is surprisingly little support for the plywood roof at the peak of the building, and the open space below is inspiring, spanning 36 x 36 feet with no trusses or beams. It is used for exhibits and the work of the Nakashima Foundation for Peace.

The entrance of the museum is home to the many awards, citations, and documents relating to Nakashima's work. Minguren translates roughly from Japanese as *People's Tool Association* and refers to a crafts movement in Japan.

Classic Nakashim style characterizes a conference table in the Minguren Museum.

A cantilevered staircase rises along an interior stonewall of the Minguren Museum. This image showcases Nakashima's adoption of traditional Japanese architecture in the exposed wooden beams, shoji screens that blur the line between indoors and outdoors, and natural colors.

GEORGE NAKASHIMA

Examples of carefully crafted door and drawer pulls by Nakashima.

Looking at the Nakashima family home from the woods.

Nakashima's son, Kevin, still lives in the family home. The stones for the original walls were gathered from the property, or along the roadside, Nakashima relates. Eventually, the family did end up purchasing one load of stone to complete the house, but most of the materials were scrounged. Wood was used "rather green," he wrote, but was found locally and was inexpensive. Today Nakashima's original furnishings are surely worth a fortune. Artwork by Ben Shahn adorns the walls and a Soleri Bell hung from the ceiling. The frames use free edges, Kevin explains, a "form my father came up with."

Inside the entryway, sliding doors conceal coats and boots. The family home, now home to son, Kevin, was built in 1947. "The old showroom was in the house. Dad really believed in living an integrated life," said his daughter, Mira Nakashima Yarnall.

A nook in the kitchen area of the house. Trademark Nakashima chairs are prominent

Left:
A nook in the Reception House.

Right:
A portion of the kitchen of the main house.

GEORGE NAKASHIMA

A barbecue center offered an early opportunity for Nakashima to play with a cantilevered roofline. The family calls this their Simpson Room.

The Mountain Villa, a guesthouse, was built in 1975. "It was the last house that dad built. He wanted it to be the *piece de la resistance*," says daughter, Mira. "He supervised every day in the building of everything."

The central room in The Mountain Villa provides a wonderful place to relax with guests.

The guest house has a traditional Japanese *genkan* or vestibule. Sliding doors provide for shoe storage.

The dining table and chairs are classic Nakashima. Shoji doors conceal a cooking center, where stove, oven, and refrigerator can be accessed.

George Nakashima 147

Nakashima-designed stools are upholstered in antique Japanese cloth, indigo dyed using the lost-wax technique.

Grandchildren's and son's names were added to the playful mosaic that surrounds a soaking tub in the guesthouse bath.

GEORGE NAKASHIMA 151

A traditional tearoom is located off the dining area in the guesthouse.

Mira Nakashima and her husband, Jonathan Yarnall, live across the street from the main complex of buildings.

A Mecca for many who make their way to Nakashima's studio, the wood shed is the lifeblood of the studio's work. Trees selected years earlier and cut in collaboration with a sawyer were cured for up to five years in a lumberyard before finding their way to the Nakashima complex, where they await the perfect commission. (continued on following 3 pages)

A little Asian flair finds its way on an otherwise utilitarian facade.

At the periphery of the property, the arched roof of a pool house forms a soaring shelter, mirrored by the arch of an adjacent utility area.

GEORGE NAKASHIMA

Bibliography

Adamson, Jeremy. *The Furniture of Sam Maloof*. Washington, D.C.: Smithsonian American Art Museum, 2001.

Maloof, Sam. *Sam Maloof: Woodworker*. Tokyo: Kodansha International Ltd., 1983.

Nakashima, George. *The Soul of a Tree*. Tokyo: Kodansha International Ltd., 1981.

Nakashima, Mira. *Nature, Form & Spirit: The Life and Legacy of George Nakashima*. New York: Harry N. Abrams, Inc., 2003.

Stone, Michael A. *Contemporary American Woodworkers*. Layton, UT: Gibbs M. Smith, Inc.